This is my
tractor

Written by Chris Oxlade
Photography by Christine Lalla

SEA-TO-SEA

Mankato Collingwood London

This edition first published in 2008 by
Sea-to-Sea Publications
1980 Lookout Drive
North Mankato
Minnesota 56003

Printed in China

Library of Congress Cataloging in Publication Data

Oxlade, Chris.
   This is my tractor / by Chris Oxlade.
      p.cm. -- (Mega machine drivers)
   ISBN 978-1-59771-106-7
   1. Tractors--Juvenile literature. I. Title.

TL233.15.)95 2007
631.3'72--dc22

2006051284

9 8 7 6 5 4 3 2

Published by arrangement with the Watts Publishing Group Ltd, London.
Editor: Jennifer Schofield
Designer: Jemima Lumley
Photography: Christine Lalla, unless otherwise acknowledged
Tractor driver: Charlie Murray

Acknowledgments:
John Deere: 7, 15, 17b, 18, 19, 20, 21, 23, 25, 26, 27b
The Publisher would like to thank Steve Mitchell, Charlie Murray,
and all at John Deere for their help producing this book.

Every attempt has been made to clear copyright.
Should there be any inadvertent omission please
apply to the publisher for rectification.

Contents

My tractor and me

Hello! I am a tractor driver.
This is my tractor.

My tractor helps me
do jobs on my farm.

>Tractor power

All the parts of my tractor are worked by the engine.

∧*This is the engine.*
It is big and powerful.

The engine needs fuel to work.
The fuel is stored in the fuel tank.

◁ *The tank is made of very tough plastic.*

> Wheels and tyres

The giant wheels let me drive over muddy and bumpy fields.

∧ *My tractor's wheels are almost as tall as me!*

The tires have a chunky pattern so they can grip in the mud.

Adding machines

I often put special machines onto my tractor for jobs on the farm.

Farming machines go on the back of the tractor.

This spinning rod from the engine makes the machines work.

Some machines are very heavy.
This weight at the front stops the
tractor from tipping backward.

▶ Picking up

This is how I pick up a farm machine.

◀ *First I back up to the machine.*

▶ *Then I attach the machine to the tractor.*

▼ *Now I can lift up the machine to carry it along. This machine is called a disk harrow.*

In my cab

I sit in the cab to drive my tractor. The cab keeps me warm and dry.

cab

> *The cab has big windows so I can see all around me when I am driving.*

∨ *At night I turn on the bright spotlights on my cab.*

> Cab controls

The cab is full of controls for driving and working different machines.

> *I use the steering wheel to turn to the left or right.*

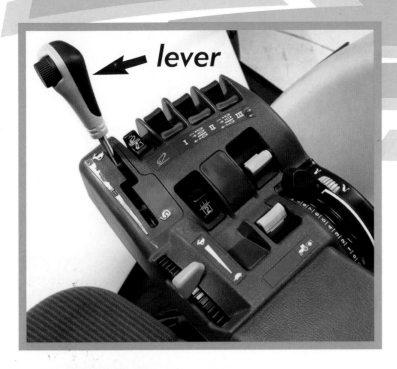

lever

< *This lever lets me drive along at different speeds.*

∧ *There are lots of switches here. Some work the tractor's lights. Some work farm machines.*

Collecting hay

Today, I am collecting hay from my fields.

△ *This machine is called a baler. It rolls hay into bales.*

I carry the bales with a bale fork on the front of the tractor.

Now I am towing away the bales on a dray.

▶ Plowing

We use a tractor to plow a field.

▲ The tractor carries the plow to the field.

◀ This part is called a plow blade.

▽The plow blades churn up the soil.

 More tractors

Here are some of the
other machines I drive.

This giant tractor has
tracks instead of wheels.

A combine harvester collects crops from my fields.

> Be a tractor driver

It takes lots of practice
to become a tractor driver.

▽ *You have to learn how to drive
the tractor safely along bumpy
farm tracks and on the roads.
You also have to practice towing
trailers and drays.*

You have to learn about all the tractor's levers and switches.

You have to learn how to work farm machines and how to put them onto the tractor.

▷ Tractor parts

spotlights

cab

window

engine
(inside)

weight

tire

fuel tank

▷ Word bank

disk harrow—a machine that breaks up soil and makes it level

fuel—the liquid that burns inside an engine

hay—grass that has been cut and dried

plow—a machine that churns up soil in a field

spotlight—a light that makes a beam like a powerful flashlight

tracks—the loops of metal or rubber links some tractors have.

trailer—a vehicle that is pulled along by a tractor

Web fun

John Deere has a great website, especially for children. Log on at:

http://www.deere.com/en_US/compinfo/kidscorner/home.html

Index

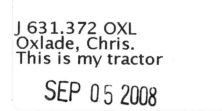